W9-CEK-891

essential careers™

CAREERS AS A
COMMISSIONED
SALES
REPRESENTATIVE

MINDY MOZER

RosenPUBLISHING

NEW YORK

Published in 2014 by The Rosen Publishing Group, Inc.
29 East 21st Street, New York, NY 10010

First Edition

Library of Congress Cataloging-in-Publication Data

Mozer, Mindy.
Careers as a commissioned sales representative/Mindy Mozer. — First edition.
    pages cm. — (Essential careers)
Includes bibliographical references and index.
Audience: Grade 7 to 12.
ISBN 978-1-4777-1794-3 (library binding)
1. Sales personnel—Juvenile literature. 2. Selling—Vocational guidance—Juvenile literature. I. Title.
HF5439.5.M69 2014
658.85023—dc23

                                                                2013013521

Manufactured in Malaysia

CPSIA Compliance Information: Batch #W14YA: For further information, contact Rosen Publishing, New York, New York, at 1-800-237-9932.

contents

INTRO

A Volkswagen salesman helps a customer purchase his new Passat. People who work on commission need to know a lot about the products they are selling so that they can help customers purchase the product that is right for them.

DUCTION

The employee worked on paperwork quietly at his desk until the customers walked into the showroom. He approached them to see why they were visiting the automobile dealership that day. The customers explained to the salesman that they needed a car that could accommodate their growing family. They often carted around sporting equipment, so they needed a vehicle with ample storage space. They also wanted a car with heated seats and satellite radio.

The salesman showed them several vehicles that fit their needs and explained the unique features of each one. He answered their questions and accompanied them on a test drive. He then worked with them on financing and payment options and signed them up for any rebates and special offers for which they qualified. He explained the dealership's warranty policy and service options. He processed the sale and arranged a date for the car to be picked up.

For his work, the salesman received a commission. A commission is money based on the percentage of a sale. Some people are paid only on commission. That means they are paid only when they make a sale, so their salary is completely based on their performance. Some people receive a salary and earn commissions, too. These people usually earn a lower base salary than people who are just paid a salary and don't receive commissions because the commissions can make up the difference. Some people also earn bonuses on top of commissions for meeting sales goals. For example, the car salesman may earn extra money for selling a certain number of cars a month.

An advantage of working on commission is that the person who works the hardest or is the best at what he or she does is generally paid the most. Another advantage is that there is an unlimited amount of money a person can earn. But people who are paid on commission must work hard to make money. Unlike people who are paid a salary, if they don't sell anything, their income suffers. This makes it challenging to budget month to month. Also, the general public sometimes views people who work on commission as being pushy or forcing sales on reluctant or uninterested customers just so they can get paid.

Many types of jobs pay commissions. These jobs all have one thing in common—they involve selling a product or service that people or businesses need as well as want. The products sold on commission include advertising, cars, furniture, clothes, appliances, real estate, computers, insurance, financial advice, travel packages, and loans. Even when the economy is not doing well, these jobs are in demand. Businesses still advertise and purchase updated computers during economic downturns, and individuals still need financial advice, insurance, and places to live.

People who work on commission need to know a lot about both the products they are selling and the products they are competing against. The car salesman likely would not have made the sale if he hadn't been able to show the customers a vehicle that matched their needs. Although the job can be stressful, working on commission is potentially very rewarding. People who work on commission only need to look at their paychecks to see the results of their hard work.

chapter 1

ADVERTISING SALES

Advertising sales agents or representatives sell advertising space. That space can be on a billboard, in a newspaper, on television, on the radio, and even on the Internet or a tablet computer like an iPad. But before advertising sales agents can get a billboard placed on a busy road, they have to find clients who have something to advertise. Then the sales agent has to build a relationship with the client and learn as much as possible about the client's products and his or her competition. The sales agent also has to know the target market, which is the group of customers the business is hoping to reach, and the geographic area in which the product is sold.

After doing all of this research, the sales agent sets up a meeting with the client. The agent then explains how specific types of advertising will help the client sell his or her product. This is usually done with an advertising proposal. An advertising proposal includes sample advertisements and estimates for how much it would cost to place those sample ads in various places, such as billboards, newspapers, television, and the Internet. Advertising sales agents also come up with advertising sales packages, which allow clients to buy several types of ads in one package.

This artist's rendering shows a large sign for China's news agency Xinhua. The rendering was made before the advertisement appeared in New York City's Times Square. Advertising sales agents often show clients options for how ads might look before they are placed.

Once a client has selected a proposal, an advertising sales representative then creates a contract, which outlines the cost and the work that needs to be done. The representative goes over that contract with the client, answers questions, and addresses concerns the client might have.

It is important for advertising sales agents to stay on top of the latest sales industry trends. They should keep tabs on how companies are spending their advertising dollars and in what media (print, television, Internet, radio). Sales agents are also responsible for developing sales tools, promotional plans, and media kits, which they can use when meeting with clients.

WHAT ARE THE DUTIES?

Here is a breakdown of the day-to-day activities of an advertising sales agent:

- Find potential clients. Advertising sales agents must figure out what companies might be interested in advertising their services.
- Sell the idea. Once advertising sales agents have found potential clients, they have to explain to them how advertising will help their business. They have to sell them on the idea of advertising.
- Estimate the advertising costs of different publications and then explain that to clients. For example, the cost will be different to advertise on a billboard than it will be to advertise on prime time television. The advertising sales agent has to figure out the advantages and disadvantages of all advertising outlets and then match the client's advertising needs to the right publications.
- Target the advertising. Explain to clients how specific types of advertising will help promote their

products or services in the most effective way possible. For example, it might not be a good use of resources to advertise a high school tutoring program in a publication that isn't read by high school students or their parents.

- Provide estimates. Advertising sales agents have to estimate the cost of advertising products and services in various ways and share that with clients.
- Keep track of all correspondence with clients.
- Help clients prepare the ad. This may involve showing clients options for how the ad might look, helping them figure out what the ad will say, and providing samples.
- Deliver advertising samples. Advertising samples are called proofs. These proofs must be sent to clients for approval before publication.

Advertising sales agents must listen closely to clients to come up with a successful advertising plan. Once a client has agreed to a plan, a sales agent creates a contract, which outlines the cost and the work that needs to be done.

- Prepare promotional plans, sales literature, media kits, and sales contracts.

WHAT DO ADVERTISING SALES AGENTS SELL?

Advertising sales agents sell advertising space in a number of formats:

- **Television:** Advertisements can appear on network television stations and cable stations. These ads, also known as commercials, range in length from a few seconds to one or two minutes. In some cases, companies buy longer periods of television time and produce infomercials.
- **Radio:** Advertising sales agents who work for radio stations sell radio airtime, also called radio spots. These commercials run in between music and news programming.
- **Print:** Advertisements appear in magazines, daily newspapers, weekly newspapers, and shopper guides. Advertisements can also be found in fliers and mail that is sent directly to potential buyers. The cost to advertise in print publications varies depending on the publication.
- **Billboards:** Advertising can be found on outdoor signs or posters.
- **Online:** This type of advertising, which is the promotion of products over the Internet, is experiencing the most growth. Online advertising can be found on Web sites, blogs, and social media Web sites.
- **Other locations:** Advertising sales representatives can sell advertising almost anywhere. You will see

TIPS ON HOW TO FIGURE OUT THE RIGHT CAREER FOR YOU

- What do you do well? Write down the tasks you do well. If you figure out your natural talents, your job won't feel like work.
- What products or services most interest you?
- Who do you admire? Make a list of who you look up to and why.
- What makes you happy? What activities are you doing that make you the happiest?
- What's your work style? Do you like to work under deadline pressure with strict guidelines, or do you prefer a flexible work schedule and environment? Which environment allows you to do your best work?
- What type of sales interests you? Do you prefer selling products over the phone or in person?
- How much do you want to travel? Do you want to work in a small town or a large city?
- Do you like working with others? Do you want to be part of a team? Do you like to share ideas with others and solve problems in groups, or would you rather work alone?
- Do you want to work on weekends? If you want to be home every night and on the weekends, find a job with regular hours that doesn't require overtime and weekend work.
- Do you want to work with customers? Are you good at talking to people and representing a company?
- How well do you handle stress? Do you thrive under stress or prefer a more laid-back job?
- How much money do you want to make? Consider how much money you need to meet your expectations and the requirements of a future family.

ads on signs in sports arenas, on the sides of buildings, on buses and taxis, and on flags pulled by airplanes. You will even find them in places such as public bathrooms.

WORK ENVIRONMENT

Advertising sales agents spend most of their time out of the office, visiting clients and potential clients where they work. When they are in the office, they spend time contacting clients to set up appointments and doing background work on their accounts. They may be employed by big advertising firms or small companies, or they may run their own business.

Advertising sales agents generally work full-time, and many work more than forty hours a week. Some advertising sales agents work on weekends, nights, and holidays because they have to be available to meet with clients whenever it is most convenient for them. Some companies set monthly sales quotas. In order to meet those quotas, advertising sales agents may have to work long hours.

EDUCATION AND TRAINING

A high school diploma is required for most entry-level advertising sales positions. Some companies like applicants to have

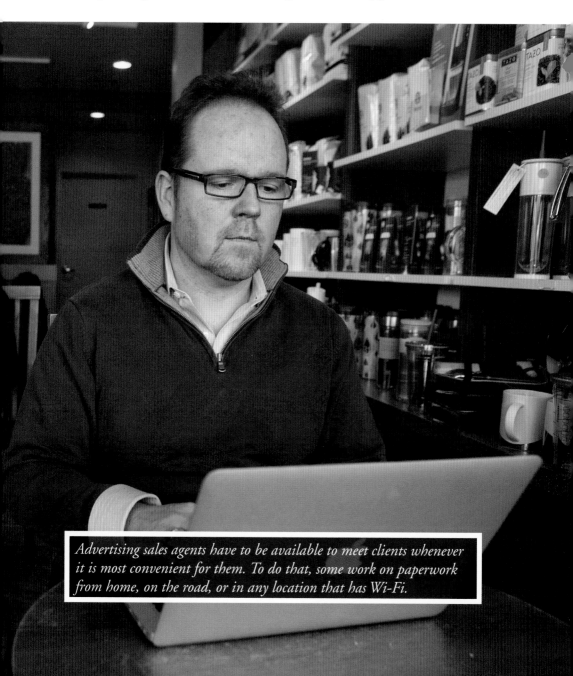

Advertising sales agents have to be available to meet clients whenever it is most convenient for them. To do that, some work on paperwork from home, on the road, or in any location that has Wi-Fi.

a bachelor's degree with courses in business, marketing, communications, and advertising. An advertising sales agent must be able to communicate effectively and be comfortable working with people.

Most of the training for an advertising sales position happens on the job with an experienced sales manager teaching a new sales agent. The experienced professional shows a new person how to make sales calls, interact with clients, create advertising proposals, and follow up with clients. Some companies send employees through training sessions so that they can learn about target markets and selling techniques. Those who do well as advertising sales agents may be promoted to managerial positions such as sales manager or supervisor.

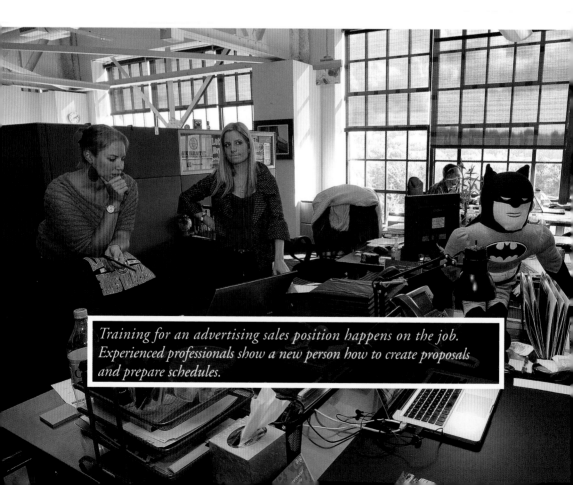

Training for an advertising sales position happens on the job. Experienced professionals show a new person how to create proposals and prepare schedules.

SALARY

The salary of advertising sales agents can fall within a wide range because agents are paid based on their performance. Most employers pay advertising sales agents a combination of a salary, commission, and bonuses. Bonuses can be based on an individual's performance, the performance of all sales workers in a group, or the performance of the entire sales firm. For the latest salary information for this position and all the other jobs described in this book, consult the U.S. Bureau of Labor Statistics' online *Occupational Outlook Handbook*.

FUTURE OUTLOOK

The area that is growing the most in the advertising sales field is digital media. Digital media includes ads that are made to be viewed on cell phones, laptops and PCs, and tablets. Advertisements on Web sites will also continue to be in demand in the future. This area is called Internet publishing. Internet publishing allows clients to target their ads to certain populations because Web sites are often associated with particular types of products (cars, computers, books, music, movies, fashion, etc.) or with people who have particular interests and consumer tastes and tendencies. Although print advertising is expected to decline, experts predict there will be growth in newspapers selling online advertising space. Advertising on television and radio is expected to remain strong.

chapter 2

Retail Sales

Have you ever gone into a clothing store and been greeted at the entrance by an employee? The employee then helps you find clothing in the right size, the right style, and the right price range. He or she may bring various sizes to the dressing room and make suggestions about the right fit and color. The employee is a retail sales worker. Retail sales workers sell products, such as clothing, furniture, and cars. Their job is to help customers find what they are looking for and then sell them a product. They are sometimes paid on commission, so the more they sell, the more money they make.

Retail sales employees work in a variety of stores. You will find them in clothing stores and shoe stores. Others sell cars, cosmetics, electronics, and furniture. The primary responsibility of a retail sales worker is to help customers find items to buy and then process the sale of those items. Retail sales workers often operate the cash register, so they have to know how to count change, handle exchanges, and process coupons. Some retail sales workers take cash and checks that customers use to pay for items and deposit them in the bank at the end of the day. After customers have paid for their items, retail sales workers generally put the items into a bag. Retail sales workers also stock shelves, take inventory, mark price tags, and put merchandise on display in an attractive way.

Retail sales workers need to have a good understanding of the products they are selling, especially if they are selling expensive items such as cars. A car salesperson has to be able to talk about a car's features and how those features are different from other cars. A car salesperson must also understand car warranties and financing. Some retail sales workers might sell car parts and equipment in automotive parts stores or car dealerships. They work with customers by taking their orders and explaining pricing. They may also take inventory one or more times a year.

WHAT ARE THE DUTIES?

Here is a breakdown of the day-to-day activities of a retail sales agent:

- Greet customers and figure out what the customer is interested in buying.
- Find merchandise that matches the customer's wants and needs.
- Explain the merchandise to the customer.
- Answer questions about the merchandise.
- Show how a product works. For example, if a retail sales worker is selling a car, he or she might show the customer the unique features.
- Total the merchandise and accept payment.
- Use scanners, cash registers, and calculators to ring up items that customers buy. Accept payment, process credit cards, and give change if needed.
- Answer questions about the company's policies, including exchange policies, promotions, and security practices.

WHAT DO RETAIL SALES AGENTS SELL?

- **Clothing:** These employees work in clothing and clothing accessory stores. They help customers find the right outfit or accessory, bring clothing to dressing rooms for customers to try on, and then process the final sale.

Retail sales agents work in clothing stores and boutiques. They answer questions about merchandise, ring up items, and accept payment.

- **Automobiles:** These employees work in car dealer-ships, independent car businesses, or used car shops. They need to have a basic understanding of how the cars they are selling work and their unique features. They may also work with customers on obtaining financing and trade-ins for their old vehicles.
- **Furniture:** These employees work in furniture stores or large warehouse stores. They need to understand

how the furniture is made and the materials the furniture is made of. They may also process sales and help customers with financing and delivery.

- **Jewelry:** These employees work in jewelry stores or jewelry sections of large department stores. They need to understand different types of jewelry and the different

Retail sales agents who sell computers must know about ever-changing technology so that they can help customers understand the latest features and capabilities and select the computer that is best for them.

metals and gemstones jewelry can be made of. Those selling diamonds have to understand diamond quality and standards.

- **Appliances:** These employees work in appliance and home stores. They need to understand how various appliances work. They also help customers with financing, extended warranties, and trade-ins of old appliances. They process sales and arrange for delivery.

- **Electronics:** These employees work in stores that sell everything from televisions to cell phones. They need to stay on top of the latest consumer trends so that they can help customers pick the right device for their particular needs. They have to be able to operate the electronic devices they are selling so that they can explain the features to customers. Like other retail sales agents, they help customers with financing, warranties, and delivery.

- **Computers/office supplies:** These employees work in specialty computer stores or big-box retail stores. Like electronics salespeople, they have to know how to run a large selection of computers

This customer gets assistance from a retail sales agent as he shops for a Mother's Day gift at a jewelry kiosk in a shopping mall.

so that they can help customers decide which computer is best for them. They have to understand computer terminology and stay on top of the latest trends. They help customers with financing and warranties and may even ring up the sale.

- **Sports and outdoor equipment:** These employees work in specialty stores or big sporting goods stores. They need to be experts in sporting equipment. Some may specialize in certain areas, such as camping, climbing, hunting, or fishing equipment.

- **Cosmetics:** These employees work in cosmetic stores or large department stores. They work directly with customers, explaining the options and the benefits of each product. In some cases, these employees help customers test the cosmetics in the store.

QUALITIES YOU NEED TO WORK IN SALES

- **Customer-service skills:** Retail sales workers must have strong customer-service skills. They need to be able to explain products to customers, make recommendations, and answer questions.
- **People skills:** Retail sales workers need to have outgoing personalities that make people want to interact with them. They need to be able to ask the right questions so that they can help customers find the right products.
- **Persistence:** Retail sales workers can't give up or be easily discouraged.
- **Confidence:** Retail sales workers need to be confident in what they are selling so that customers trust their advice and opinion.
- **Listening skills:** Retail sales workers need to listen to customers so that they can help them find the right product.
- **Flexibility:** Retail sales workers may have to work weekends, nights, and holidays. Their shifts may change each week, so they have to remain flexible.
- **Product knowledge:** Good salespeople understand the products they are selling. They understand the competition and are able to communicate the differences to customers.
- **Selling skills:** Retail sales workers must be persuasive. They must clearly and effectively explain the benefits of the merchandise they are selling.
- **Attention to detail:** Retail sales workers need to be able to help customers navigate rebates, sales, special offers, financing, and warranties.

WORK ENVIRONMENT

Retail sales employees generally work inside stores or shopping malls unless they are selling outdoor items. Car salespeople may go in and out of the showroom to show customers the various cars on the lot and join them for test drives. Retail sales workers tend to stand for most of their work shift. Sales workers work day shifts, night shifts, weekends, and holidays. November and December are busy times for sales workers because of the holiday shopping season. February can be a busy time for jewelry sales because of Valentine's Day. Retail sales employees can work full-time or part-time, depending on the business.

EDUCATION AND TRAINING

A retail sales position is one that can be learned on the job. Most employers want applicants to have a high school diploma. Employees who have taken some post–high school classes in business are preferred. And it is helpful for those employees selling electronics to have some technical knowledge of the products.

New retail sales workers get on-the-job training, which can last anywhere from a few days to several months. Those working for national companies may go through a formal training program. Workers are trained on how to greet customers, how to help customers find the product that is right for them, the store's policies, store security, how to operate the cash register, how to process credit cards, how to arrange for deliveries, and how to help customers with financing.

New employees might also receive specialized training in the products they are selling. Those employees selling computers, for example, will have to learn the technical specifications and operations of various models. Retail sales workers may also get specialized training after they have been

Some sales agents receive specialized training in the products they are selling because they have to be able to explain the technical features to customers.

on the job for a while to update their skills and ensure that they have the latest information on the products they are selling.

Retail sales workers have opportunities to move into managerial positions. Or they may have the chance to switch to another department, with the potential to make higher commissions. For example, a department store sales worker will make a higher commission selling high-end jewelry than he or she will selling clothes.

SALARY

The amount of money a retail sales worker gets paid depends on what the worker is selling. Those who get paid on commission make more money if they are selling a higher-priced product because they make a percentage of the sales. Some retail sales workers are paid hourly wages. Some get a combination of both.

FUTURE OUTLOOK

According to the U.S. Bureau of Labor Statistics (BLS), employment of retail salespersons is predicted to grow. Population growth will increase retail sales, and workers will be needed to fill the growing number of sales positions. Warehouse clubs and supercenters are expected to see the biggest growth. Employment in this area is expected to grow 51 percent between 2010 and 2020. Retail sales opportunities in department stores, however, are predicted to decline. The same is true for car salespeople because consumers are driving cars longer than they used to before trading them in or replacing them.

chapter 3

REAL ESTATE SALES

Have you ever noticed "For Sale" signs on the front lawns of homes? The signs usually list the person who is representing the sellers of the property, the company that person works for, and a contact number for potential buyers to get more information. The person who represents the buyers and sellers of property is called a real estate agent or a real estate broker. His or her job is to help people buy, sell, and rent property.

The difference between a real estate agent and a real estate broker is that a broker is licensed to manage his or her own real estate business. Brokers sell real estate owned by others. They may also help rent or manage properties. They run a real estate office and oversee the work of sales agents. A sales agent must work with a broker. Sometimes they work with a broker on a contract basis, earning a portion of the commission from each property. The broker then gets the rest of the commission.

People hire real estate agents and brokers because buying or selling property is complicated. Buyers want to make sure they are paying a fair price for a home. Sellers want to make sure they are receiving a fair price for a home. A real estate agent helps with the negotiations. There is also a lot of paperwork involved, and a real estate agent can help buyers and sellers fill out and file everything properly.

Real estate brokers and agents can work with either the buyer or the seller. When their clients are buyers, they meet with them to figure out what type of property they are interested in buying, how much money they want to spend, and where they want the property to be located. When their clients are sellers, they help them decide how much money to ask for, where to advertise the property, and how to show the property to best advantage.

Real estate brokers and sales agents must understand the real estate market in their area. They need to know what homes in the area are selling for. They need to know how close homes are to shopping centers and schools. They need to be familiar with the area's crime rate. They also need to understand how to help buyers get financing so that they can purchase homes.

WHAT ARE THE DUTIES?

Here is a breakdown of the day-to-day activities of a real estate agent or broker:

• Find people who want to sell, buy, or rent property.

Real estate agents help people buy, sell, and rent property. People hire them because buying and selling property is an extremely complicated process.

- Help people selling property figure out how much money to sell it for based on the condition of the property, its location, and how much other, similar properties in the neighborhood are selling for.
- Help people buying property figure out how much money to offer for purchase, based on the condition of the property, its location, and how much similar, nearby properties are selling for.
- Have a good understanding of property pricing in the area and how it has changed over time.
- Come up with a list of properties for sale, including details about the property, its location, and its special features.
- Let people know the property is for sale by listing it in advertisements and on the Internet.
- Take buyers and renters to visit properties.
- Present purchase offers to sellers.
- Negotiate prices with buyers and sellers.
- Prepare contracts and other paperwork when a purchase price has been agreed upon.
- Make sure buyers and sellers abide by the terms of the contract.
- Stay current on financing options, types of available mortgages, and real estate laws.

WHAT DO REAL ESTATE BROKERS AND AGENTS SELL?

- **Residential property:** Most real estate brokers and agents sell residential property, which is property where people live. This can include homes where a single family lives, apartments where many families live, townhouses, and condominiums.
- **Commercial property:** Agents and brokers sell commercial property, which is property where

Many real estate agents sell residential property. Part of their job involves walking buyers through homes for sale.

businesses are located. The property is classified that way by a town or city because governments like to keep commercial property within designated districts. A family, for example, would not be allowed to live in a building designated as commercial property.

- **Industrial property:** Some brokers and agents sell industrial property, which is property used for warehouse or factory space, where people make or store products.

- **Agricultural property:** A small number of agents and brokers sell agricultural property where farms are located.

WORK ENVIRONMENT

Real estate brokers and agents work in offices. Many are self-employed, so they may work in a one-person business or out of their home. Some work for large companies and may work in large offices. There are national real estate companies

WHAT IS A CERTIFICATION EXAM LIKE?

Here are some sample questions from New York's real estate sales-person practice exam:

1. Jane is a broker and accepts a $3,000 deposit. What should she do with the deposit?
   a. Place it in her personal checking account.
   b. Place it in her business operating account immediately.
   c. Place it in her escrow account immediately.
   d. Place it in a safety deposit box.

2. Which of the following duties does not require real estate licensure in New York State?
   a. Negotiating the exchange of real property for others.
   b. Renting units for several different owners.
   c. Auctioning real property.
   d. Sale of business where there is no real property.

3. With regard to the resale of cooperative property for another, which of the following is necessary?
   a. A minimum of a salesperson license.
   b. A minimum of a broker license.
   c. A stockbroker's license.
   d. No license.

4. The listing salesperson must accept payment directly from the:
   a. Seller.
   b. Cooperating broker.
   c. Employing broker.
   d. Customer.

Answers: 1. C; 2. D; 3. A; 4. C

that have representatives all over the United States. Those representatives pay a fee to be affiliated with the real estate organization.

Real estate brokers and agents spend a lot of time out in the field, visiting homes, meeting with clients, showing properties to customers, and visiting properties that are for sale. Because the job requires them to show properties to clients, brokers and agents often work weeknights and weekends because that is when clients are free. It is also important for brokers and agents to network to meet new clients. Networking may involve attending community meetings and events. Agents can work part-time or full-time. Some who work part-time do real estate work on the side while working other full-time jobs.

EDUCATION AND TRAINING

Real estate brokers and agents are required to have a high school diploma. Those with a college degree are more marketable.

Some real estate agents sell agricultural property where farms are located. This lot of 127 acres (51 hectares) sold for more than $1 million.

Some colleges and universities offer courses in real estate. Courses in finance, business, and marketing are also helpful for real estate brokers and agents to have.

In the United States, real estate agents and brokers must be licensed. The license requirements vary by state, but basic requirements include completing courses about real estate and passing an exam. Candidates must be eighteen years old to qualify. Some states require candidates to pass a background check. In Texas, for example, people must take 180 hours in real estate courses before being eligible to apply for a license. Candidates must then pass an exam. In Florida, a candidate must take sixty-three hours of coursework before submitting an application for a license.

To become a licensed broker, candidates need one to three years of experience as a licensed sales agent. They will also be required to complete additional classroom training. In some states, a bachelor's degree will take the place of additional training or experience. Agents and brokers must renew their licenses every two to four years, depending on the state where they work. They may need to take additional educational courses to renew their license.

Some colleges may offer a certificate in a real estate program, which can be done in a traditional classroom or be completed online. Such programs teach students the basic concepts and techniques required for an entry-level position. Colleges also offer courses that are needed to obtain a real estate broker and salesperson license.

INTERNSHIP PROGRAMS

Some colleges offer real estate internship programs where students can work alongside an experienced real estate agent or broker and apply the lessons they have learned in the classroom to real-life situations. Some real estate firms may use the internship program as a way to find future employees.

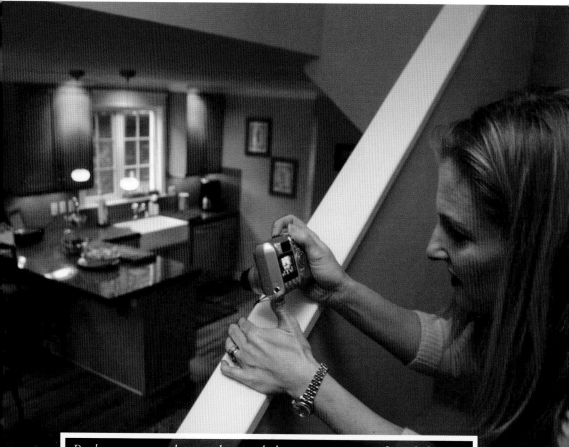

Real estate agents have to let people know a property is for sale by listing it in advertisements and on the Internet. Many agents include pictures with the listing.

SALARY

Real estate sales agents and brokers earn most of their money from commissions on sales. Commissions are divided among agents who represent the buyers and sellers and the brokers for each side. An agent's income can change as economic conditions change. During good economic times, people may buy and sell more property. During bad economic times, a real estate sales agent's income may be lower.

FUTURE OUTLOOK

There will always be jobs in the area of real estate because there will always be people who want to own their own homes and companies that require office space, retail space, and manufacturing facilities. But the health of the real estate business depends on the economy. When the economy is doing well, people will be interested in buying their own homes or starting their own businesses. When the economy is not doing well, fewer people will want to move and purchase property and companies will pull back on spending, expansion, and capital investment.

In addition, real estate can be a competitive field. New agents face competition from experienced agents. Agents who have strong ties to the community and a carefully constructed and maintained network of clients tend to do the best, especially during tough economic times.

chapter 4

INSURANCE SALES

I magine what would happen if a tornado struck your neighborhood and your house and all of your belongings were destroyed. Where would you get the money to buy a new house and replace the things that used to be in your house?

That is why people have insurance, which protects them from big losses. People pay a certain amount of money each month or year toward a type of insurance. In return, the insurance company will pay them a certain amount of money if they experience an unexpected event. There are different types of insurance that protect against different things. Auto insurance will pay for car accidents. Health insurance is designed to help pay doctor bills if someone gets sick.

Insurance sales agents sell these different types of insurance. Agents may specialize in one specific type of insurance, such as health insurance, or they may sell many different types of insurance. An agent contacts customers, explains insurance plan options, and then helps customers pick the right kind of insurance for them. Some clients do their own research about the type of insurance they want to purchase. They then go to an insurance agent when they are ready to buy. Some agents also help their clients with other services, including financial planning and retirement planning.

Captive agents are insurance sales agents who work for one insurance company. They only sell policies provided by that company. Independent insurance agents sell policies from different companies. They assess their clients' needs and then match the policies to those needs.

WHAT ARE THE DUTIES?

Here is a breakdown of the day-to-day activities of an insurance agent:

- Contact clients to see if they are interested in purchasing insurance.
- Interview clients to see what type of insurance coverage they might need.
- Explain the different insurance policies available.
- Work with clients to determine their current insurance coverage and suggest ways that it can be improved.

Insurance agents are sometimes the first on the scene after a disaster, such as a tornado or hurricane. These agents help clients get reimbursed for the damage to or loss of property.

- Customize insurance plans for people.
- Keep detailed records on insurance policies and clients. Track when insurance policies are up for renewal.
- Help people with insurance collect money if they need to place a claim.

WHAT DO INSURANCE AGENTS SELL?

- **Property insurance:** This type of insurance protects people from risks to their property, such as fire, theft, and weather damage. There are different types of property insurance, including homeowners insurance, flood insurance, and earthquake insurance.
- **Homeowners insurance:** This type of insurance covers places where people live, but it also includes coverage for accidents that happen on a person's property. For example, if a home catches on fire, homeowners insurance will most likely pay the owner money so that he or she can build a new home. Homeowners insurance will also cover expenses if someone slips and falls on your front porch.
- **Renters insurance:** This type of insurance is for people who rent their home or apartment. For example, if an apartment catches on fire, the owner of the apartment will likely have insurance to cover the cost of the building. But that insurance doesn't cover the cost of the renter's belongings inside the apartment. That is why renters purchase renters insurance, so they can get reimbursed if the home is destroyed or broken into and their belongings are stolen.
- **Specialty home insurance:** This insurance covers seasonal or vacation homes.

- **Auto insurance:** Most states require drivers to have a minimum amount of auto insurance to legally drive a vehicle. This insurance will cover money paid to another driver if a person is in an accident

This insurance agent explains health care options to clients. People typically pick a health insurance plan based on what they expect their medical needs will be in the future.

and found to be at fault. People can also purchase auto insurance to cover damages to their own vehicle.

- **Health insurance:** Most adults get health insurance for themselves and their families through their jobs. Health insurance covers visits to the doctor, medical procedures, hospitalization, and prescription medicine. Health insurance plans vary greatly and may depend on how much people pay for that plan. People pick a plan based on how often they get sick and expect to need medical care.

- **Life insurance:** This insurance pays a sum of money to someone designated by the policyholder after the policyholder dies. It is used to support the policyholder's family or pay for funeral expenses. The amount of money the insurance pays depends on the type of plan an individual purchases.

- **Long-term care insurance:** This type of insurance covers the cost of medical care and assisted living for senior citizens. Assisted living is when a senior citizen

INSURANCE STORIES

One of the first calls Iowa farmer Mike Calderwood made after a severe thunderstorm blew over two grain bins, which then struck his semitrailer, was to his insurance agent. "My first reaction was that I'd better get things rolling to get those bins rebuilt, and that I was glad it wasn't my house," Calderwood told *Farm Industry News*. "I was also very glad that we had good insurance and a good insurance agent to get things rebuilt in a timely manner."

The same thing happened after Hurricane Sandy, which struck portions of the Northeast in October 2012. By December, 360,000 claims were submitted in New York with reports of 305,000 homes destroyed just in that state.

Insurance agents play an important role in the aftermath of any natural disaster. They are the people who can help those with property damage get money to rebuild. One problem, though, is that insurance can be complicated and not every disaster is covered under a policy. In the case of Hurricane Sandy, some homeowners were not covered for flood damage, which resulted after the hurricane hit.

Those who become insurance agents will be relied upon after both natural disasters and personal loss. They need to be ready to help at all times.

lives in a place where there are people to help him or her with daily activities, like bathing or getting dressed.

- **Disability insurance:** This insurance provides money for people who are not able to work because of a short-term or long-term injury, illness, or other health issue.

WORK ENVIRONMENT

Most insurance sales agents work in offices. They spend a lot of their workday traveling to meet with clients. Some may work alone or with a handful of others in small agencies. Others may work for large insurance companies. An insurance sales agent often works weekends and evenings because he or she meets with his or her clients at times most convenient for them. Insurance sales agents also have to be available when clients need to process a claim. For example, if there is a big ice storm that causes damage to homes and vehicles, insurance agents need to help their clients document damage and file paperwork in the hours after the storm.

Insurance covers damage from unexpected accidents. An agent inspects damage to a Ford Explorer that slid off an icy road and crashed into the backyard of a house.

EDUCATION AND TRAINING

Most insurance sales agents have a high school diploma. Many have a bachelor's degree, with courses concentrated in business, finance, and economics. Insurance sales agents learn from other agents. Many employers have new agents work with experienced agents to gain a good understanding of how the business works. Employers may also send insurance sales agents to continuing education classes to stay current with the latest changes to tax laws and other state and federal regulations.

Insurance sales agents must have a license in the state in which they work. To get a license, applicants have to complete specified courses and pass state insurance licensing exams. Some states require agents to take continuing education courses every two years in order to stay current in the field. Insurance sales agents can also get certified in certain aspects of insurance.

An insurance agent works on a claim report in Colorado Springs, Colorado, after a forest fire damaged a neighborhood.

Certification is not required for a license, but it may give an agent an advantage over other agents. For example, an associate in general insurance (AINS) designation indicates people have a superior understanding of insurance principles, practices, policies, and coverage.

SALARY

Insurance sales agents are often paid by commission only. Some are paid a salary as well as a commission, while others are paid a salary only. When agents meet their sales goals, they may also earn a bonus. Insurance sales agents may make a bigger percentage on the sale when they sell new policies rather than merely renewing existing policies.

FUTURE OUTLOOK

When the economy grows, the insurance industry grows as well, as does the demand for insurance sales agents. The Internet has changed the nature of the work for insurance agents because some clients do their own research and compare insurance plans online before approaching an agent. But insurance can be complicated, and agents are still needed to help clients find just the right insurance package at the right price, explain the legal and technical terms to clients, and complete all the significant paperwork that is generated by every insurance policy and claim. In addition, as the North American population ages, more and more insurance agents will be needed to sell health insurance and long-term insurance.

chapter 5

PERSONAL FINANCIAL ADVISING

Have you ever saved up your allowance in order to buy something and then changed your mind? Perhaps you talked to friends and your parents about what you should do with the money. Should you put it in your savings account? Should you spend it? Should you loan it to a friend who asked you if he could borrow some money? Should you invest it in the stock market or in a start-up business? Personal financial advisers help people make these decisions by giving financial advice to them.

Personal financial advisers first figure out the financial needs of people and then help them invest their money accordingly, purchase insurance, and understand tax laws (because some investments may require a client to pay additional money in taxes). Personal financial advisers can help people plan for short-term goals, such as a big vacation, or long-term goals, like retirement. Personal financial advisers figure out what investments will help clients reach their goals most quickly or most safely. After a client picks an investment, a personal financial adviser then invests the money.

But the adviser's work is not finished after investing the money. A personal financial adviser has to keep tabs on the investment to make sure it is meeting the client's goals. If the investment isn't meeting the goals, a personal financial adviser makes adjustments. In addition, a client's goals may change. That will require a personal financial adviser to make changes to the investment plan to match the new goals.

Personal financial advisers suggest savings and investment strategies and opportunities, help people identify their financial needs and goals, and guide them through the intricacies of tax laws.

Personal financial advisers may specialize in one area, such as retirement planning, or they may work with clients in many areas (such as planning for college expenses, estate planning, and saving for a second or vacation home). Some may also actively buy and sell stocks and bonds on behalf of their clients. Private bankers or wealth managers are personal financial advisers who manage a collection of investments, called a portfolio, for individuals.

WHAT ARE THE DUTIES?

Here is a breakdown of the day-to-day activities of a personal financial adviser:

- Discuss financial goals with clients.
- Explain investment options to clients, along with the potential risks and additional costs of those options.
- Recommend investment options to clients.

Personal financial advisers figure out what investments will help clients reach their goals most quickly or most safely, depending on the clients' goals, desires, and risk tolerance.

- Answer questions about investment options and risks.
- Monitor investment options selected by clients.
- Help clients plan for big expenses, such as college or retirement.

WHAT DO FINANCIAL ADVISERS SELL?

Financial advisers primarily provide advice. They develop a profile of a person's financial status and help people figure out where to put their resources in order to achieve specified short- and long-term financial goals. These are the areas a financial adviser will cover:

- **Retirement accounts:** These are accounts such as 401(k) accounts or individual retirement accounts (IRAs), which people use to save money for the years after they stop working and are no longer earning a paycheck.
- **Insurance:** Financial advisers will guide clients in insurance options and products, such as medical, life, and disability insurance.
- **Educational goals:** Financial advisers will help clients set up accounts to save for their own or their children's or grandchildren's education.
- **Taxes:** Financial advisers will help clients navigate complicated tax laws.
- **Other goals:** Financial advisers help clients save for second homes, vacations, and other expensive items.

WORK ENVIRONMENT

Personal financial advisers work in offices. Some of them are self-employed. Most work full-time. They may attend

Financial advisers have to keep tabs on investments to make sure they continue to perform well and meet a client's goals.

workshops and community events in the evenings and on the weekends to bring in new clients.

EDUCATION AND TRAINING

Personal financial advisers usually have a bachelor's degree in finance, economics, accounting, business, or mathematics. It is helpful for these employees to have taken courses in investments, taxes, estate planning, and risk management. Some personal financial advisers have a master's degree in business administration (MBA).

Personal financial advisers need to have a license or several licenses depending on the products they sell. License requirements vary, but most include successfully passing a licensing exam. Financial advisers may also need to register with the U.S. Securities and Exchange Commission (SEC).

HOW TO CALCULATE A COMMISSION

People who work on commission get a percentage of the sale of each product they sell. Commissions are sometimes the only way people are paid. Other times, people earn commissions in addition to a regular salary. Here is how to calculate a commission:

1. Figure out the total amount of the sale on which the commission will be based. That means you have to know the total amount of income that qualifies for a commission.
2. Sometimes commissions vary depending on the products being sold. For example, the sale of one item that the company is promoting might result in a larger commission than the sale of another item of lesser value.
3. Calculate the commission. If your commission is 10 percent of the total, and the total is $1,000, then your earning from commission is $100.
4. Commissions can also include additional money from bonuses. An employee may receive a bonus if he or she reaches a certain sales goal, sells a certain amount of a product, or is the company's top seller.
5. Factor in any taxes on commission. This gets complicated because the amount of taxes a person pays on a salary varies. A good rule of thumb is to look at how much money in taxes was withheld on a similar commission in an earlier paycheck.

This commission makes a financial adviser's qualifications public so that clients can make wise and informed decisions when picking an adviser.

Financial advisers can also be certified. The Certified Financial Planner Board of Standards grants the certified financial planner (CFP) designation. To earn this, financial advisers must have a bachelor's degree, have at least three years of work experience, pass an exam, and agree to follow a code of ethics. The ten-hour exam has questions about the financial planning process, insurance and risk management, employee benefits planning, taxes and retirement planning, investment and real estate planning, debt management, and fund reserves.

SALARY

Typically, financial advisers who work for firms or are self-employed get a percentage of the clients' assets that they manage. Some might also earn a commission by selling financial services products. Some may receive fees for developing a financial plan

Financial advisers provide advice. They talk to clients about retirement accounts, insurance, taxes, and education goals.

and then get an extra commission if they sell investments or insurance that is recommended in the plan. Some might just receive a salary. And some are fee-only advisers who provide advice but do not get paid for the selling of any products. This practice ensures the objectivity of their financial advice and minimizes conflicts of interest.

FUTURE OUTLOOK

The need for personal financial advisers is expected to grow because the North American population is getting older. As people approach retirement age, they look to personal financial advisers for help in managing their postemployment assets and income. Older people are also interested in estate planning, in which advisers help them decide how they will distribute their wealth (to children and grandchildren, charities, foundations, etc.) after their deaths.

chapter 6

OTHER CAREERS IN COMMISSIONED SALES

The capitalist economy is based on the buying and selling of goods and services. For this reason, there are millions of sales jobs out there. The income for many of them is based, at least in part, on commissions earned with each sale of a good or service.

WHOLESALE AND MANUFACTURING SALES REPRESENTATIVES

Have you ever wondered how stores get the products they sell? Wholesale and manufacturing sales representatives sell goods directly to businesses instead of to consumers. They work for manufacturers, wholesalers, or technical companies. They sell a range of products, from agricultural and mechanical equipment to computers and pharmaceutical goods. Some may sell food, office supplies, and clothing. Some may work with a technical expert who can explain the product in detail and answer questions.

There are two main types of wholesale and manufacturing sales representatives. Inside sales representatives work in offices. They are in charge of getting new clients and establishing the first contact with potential clients. They also take calls from people interested in buying their products. Outside sales representatives travel and visit clients and potential clients. They may show them samples and talk to customers about prices and availability of products.

WHAT ARE THE DUTIES?

Here is a breakdown of the day-to-day activities of a wholesale and manufacturing sales representative:

- Find customers by attending trade shows and by getting recommendations from current customers.
- Contact customers to learn more about the type of products they are interested in purchasing.
- Help customers select products based on their needs.
- Answer questions about prices and sales agreements.
- Negotiate prices.

Pharmaceutical sales representatives often use their cars as an office because their job involves a lot of travel to visit clients across a wide geographical area.

- Prepare sales contracts and submit orders.
- Follow-up with customers to make sure they like the products they purchased.
- Train employees on how to operate new equipment.
- Help customers display new merchandise.
- Stay up-to-date on new products.
- Prepare reports about products.

WHAT DO WHOLESALE AND MANUFACTURING SALES REPRESENTATIVES SELL?

- **Pharmaceutical sales representatives** sell medical products to health care workers. They give presentations to medical staff, and call doctors, pharmacists, and other medical professionals. They arrange appointments with medical professionals, organize conferences, and stay up-to-date on the latest medical information.
- **Agricultural sales representatives** sell products related to food and crop production. These employees need a solid background in agriculture. They have to know how equipment works and need to understand agricultural practices, such as how fertilizers affect crops.
- **Computer sales representatives** sell computer hardware and software. They are a bridge between computer companies and consumers. These sales representatives have to understand the technical components of the products they are selling. They negotiate prices and then provide technical support for the merchandise.
- **Food sales representatives** sell food products from producers and manufacturers to wholesale and retail food businesses, such as restaurants and stores. Some

may specialize and sell only certain types of food or work with only certain types of customers, such as restaurants, supermarkets, or gourmet markets.

WORK ENVIRONMENT

Some wholesale and manufacturing sales representatives may have a sales region that covers several states, which means they have to do a lot of traveling. Others might have a small territory. These sales representatives spend time on the telephone or e-mailing and video conferencing to work with customers. Most work full-time, and the job can include evening and weekend hours. Generally, however, wholesale and manufacturing sales representatives set their own schedules.

EDUCATION AND TRAINING

The amount of education needed varies depending on what the sales representative is selling. If the products are scientific or technical, such as pharmaceuticals, sales representatives must have a bachelor's degree. Many companies provide training programs for beginning employees. New hires shadow experienced employees to become familiar with products and clients.

Employees can earn either the certified professional manufacturers' representative (CPMR) certification or the certified sales professional (CSP) certification offered by the Manufacturers' Representatives Education Research Foundation. Certification involves formal training and the passing of a certification exam.

SALARY

How wholesale sales representatives are paid varies. Most receive a salary and commissions, which are based on the value of sales.

Some companies also pay bonuses based on an individual's performance or the performance of a group of workers.

FUTURE OUTLOOK

Wholesale and manufacturing sales representatives spend a portion of their job having face-to-face meetings with clients. That means this work is not likely to be outsourced to other countries. In addition, companies are hiring independent contractors to handle their sales as a way to cut costs. These independent, third-party companies then hire their own staff of sales representatives.

LOAN OFFICERS

Loan officers meet with people and businesses and decide whether to approve a loan. A loan is money that people borrow

Commercial loan officers help businesses obtain loans to expand or purchase expensive equipment, such as these John Deere tractors.

and then are expected to pay back with interest, which is an extra fee.

Loan officers use a process called underwriting to determine whether people qualify for the loans. They determine whether people will be able to pay back the money based on their income, investments, assets, expenses, and credit history. Loan officers collect information, verify financial documents, and then decide if the person qualifies for a loan. Some loan officers figure out an applicant's financial status manually. Others use computer software, which, after the financial information is entered, gives them a recommendation.

Loan officers work directly with customers, answering questions and guiding them through the application process. They also have to find customers who are interested in taking out loans and are likely to qualify.

WHAT ARE THE DUTIES?

Here is a breakdown of the day-to-day activities of loan officers:

- Find people who need a loan.
- Meet with loan applicants.
- Explain different types of loans and the terms of loans to applicants.
- Verify financial information of the applicant.

WHAT ARE THE DIFFERENT TYPES OF LOAN OFFICERS?

- **Loan collection officers** contact people who do not make their loan payments on time and work with them so that they can continue paying off the loan.

MANAGING MONEY

1. Set goals. Write down a list of financial goals and expectations during the next year and the next three years. For example, "Save $2,000 to go toward a car."
2. Figure out monthly income. How much money is available each month?
3. Figure out expenses. Make a list of monthly expenses, including rent/mortgage, credit card bills, and utilities.
4. Figure out flexible expenses, which vary month to month, such as food, clothing, and entertainment.
5. Figure out quarterly or annual expenses, such as car insurance and taxes.
6. Create a budget. Make sure expenses are less than income. If they aren't, figure out a way to reduce expenses.
7. Save. Set aside as much money as possible each month. A good guideline is to create an emergency fund that will cover three to six months of living expenses.
8. Review the budget. Look at the budget each year and make sure it is still meeting goals and expectations.

If the person still isn't able to make payments, loan collection officers will begin taking away what the person used to obtain and guarantee the loan, which is called collateral. Common types of collateral are homes and cars.

- **Loan underwriters** figure out whether a person qualifies for a loan. A borrower fills out a loan application and the underwriter evaluates the person's credit.

- **Mortgage loan officers** specialize in loans used to buy property and buildings, which are called mortgage loans. They work on loans for residential and commercial properties.
- **Commercial loan officers** specialize in loans to businesses. Businesses use loans to buy supplies, start companies, or expand. This type of loan is complicated because companies have complicated financial situations.
- **Consumer loan officers** specialize in loans to people. People take out loans to buy cars and pay for college, among other reasons. Loan officers help applicants through the process.

WORK ENVIRONMENT

Loan officers usually work in offices, although they may meet with clients at their homes or businesses. Most work full-time.

Loan officers explain different types of loans and the terms of loans to potential borrowers.

EDUCATION AND TRAINING

Loan officers need a high school diploma. Commercial loan officers generally need a bachelor's degree in business, finance, or a related field. They have to understand general business principles and know how to read financial statements so that they can analyze businesses applying for credit. Most loan officers get on-the-job training.

Mortgage loan officers must be licensed. The license is called a mortgage loan originator (MLO) license. To get it, they must complete twenty hours of coursework, pass an exam, and submit to background and credit checks. Loan officers can also get certified. The American Bankers Association and the Mortgage Bankers Association offer certification and training programs.

SALARY

Loan officers are usually paid a base salary and then earn commissions on the loans they sell.

FUTURE OUTLOOK

The amount of work loan officers have changes based on the strength of the economy. When the economy is weak, businesses and consumers wait to borrow funds, lenders are more cautious with their money, and many businesses and individuals do not qualify for loans. When the economy is strong, lending and borrowing increases.

TRAVEL AGENTS

Travel agents sell trips. This includes transportation, such as air flights, lodging, and admission to entertainment activities. This usually means looking through possible options and helping clients select the best travel package for them. Travel agents may also travel themselves and visit destinations so that they can make recommendations to clients. They visit restaurants and hotels to determine if they want to recommend those places.

Some travel agents work on only one type of travel, such as Disney vacations. Some may work only with specific groups, such as corporate clients or single (unmarried) people. Some work for tour companies and sell the company's tour packages. Most travel agents work full-time.

WHAT ARE THE DUTIES?

- Arrange trips for people traveling on business or vacation.
- Figure out a customer's schedule and needs.
- Arrange tour packages, entertainment, and day trips.
- Find transportation options.
- Calculate the cost of the trip.
- Book trips, which includes making travel, hotel, rental car, and entertainment reservations.
- Give clients all of the documents they need for their trip, including tickets.
- Help clients prepare their own documents, such as identification cards, passports, and visas.
- Help clients make new travel arrangements if changes need to be made before or during a trip.

WHAT DO TRAVEL AGENTS SELL?

Travel agents help clients arrange all aspects of travel. They sell vacation packages, all forms of transportation (airfare, buses, trains, and cruises), lodging, admission to activities, and restaurant vouchers.

EDUCATION AND TRAINING

Travel agents need a high school diploma to get started. Employers prefer people who know something about the travel industry. Community colleges and vocational schools offer classes in professional travel planning. Some colleges offer degrees in travel and tourism. Employers usually give new employees on-the-job training.

Travel agents can be certified by the Travel Institute. Earning a Certified Travel Associate (CTA) designation indicates that travel agents have demonstrated skills such as customer service and communication. People need eighteen months of experience to qualify for the CTA. They also have to complete twelve courses. After five years of experience, people can enroll in the Certified Travel Counselor (CTC) program. This includes completing courses on topics such as business planning and

Travel agents help clients arrange all aspects of travel, including plane tickets, lodging, and reservations for dining and entertainment.

financial planning. To obtain CTC certification, agents must also write a paper on a topic related to the travel field. In addition, some states require travel agents to have a business license before they can sell travel services.

SALARY

Travel agents can receive a salary if they work for tour operators or travel agencies. Some are paid a fee for booking services. Many also earn commissions for the travel packages they sell. For example, hotel chains may pay an agent a commission for getting a client to stay with them.

FUTURE OUTLOOK

The Internet is reducing the demand for travel agents because people can book their own trips online. However, people who go on group tours or specialized trips still need the help of travel agents. Businesses also continue to use the expertise of travel agents, but business travel varies with the economy and with advances in technology, such as videoconferencing.

glossary

advertising sales agent A Person who sells advertising space in publications, for television and radio, Web pages, or for custom signs.

agricultural property Land designated for farming activities.

assisted living Housing for the elderly or those with disabilities that provides nursing care, housekeeping, and meals.

broker A person who buys or sells goods for others.

commercial property Land on which or buildings in which businesses operate.

commission The money a salesperson earns based on the percentage of a sale.

digital media Content that can be transmitted on the Internet or via computer networks.

401(k) A retirement savings plan that allows employees to have a portion of their wages directly paid into an account. Some employers match employee contributions.

industrial property Land on which or buildings in which businesses manufacture products.

inside sales representative A sales representative who does not travel to the client. Instead, he or she explains the company's products over the phone, via e-mail, or through Web conferencing.

insurance A practice by which a person pays a fee and then is guaranteed money for the loss or damage of property or cars or to pay for the costs associated with illness or death.

loan officer A person who serves as the go-between for lending institutions and borrowers.

outside sales representative A person who travels and

identifies sales opportunities within a geographic area.

real estate agent The person who acts as the go-between for sellers and buyers of land or property.

real estate broker The person who, like a real estate agent, arranges property transactions but is at a higher level and is authorized to manage a real estate business.

residential property Buildings in which individuals and families live.

retail The sale of goods and services to the public.

sales The exchange of a product or service for money.

travel agent A person who sells or arranges trips or tours for customers.

wholesale sales representative A person who sells goods to businesses, government agencies, and other organizations. These goods are sold at a lower cost (the wholesale price) than they would be if they were sold directly to consumers (at the retail price).

for more information

American Academy of Financial Management (AAFM)
1670-F East Cheyenne Mountain Boulevard, Box #293
Colorado Springs, CO 80906
(504) 495-1748
Web site: http://www.aafm.us
The AAFM is an independent, worldwide board of standards
   and an accreditation council for management professionals.

American Society of Travel Agents (ASTA)
1101 King Street, Suite 200
Alexandria, VA 22314
(703) 739-2782
Web site: http://www.asta.org
The ASTA's mission is to facilitate the business of selling
   travel through effective representation, shared knowledge,
   and the enhancement of professionalism.

Association of Canadian Advertisers (ACA)
95 St. Clair Avenue West, Suite 1103
Toronto, ON M4V 1N6
Canada
(800) 565-0109
Web site: http://www.acaweb.ca
The ACA is a national, nonprofit association exclusively
   dedicated to serving the interests of companies that market
   and advertise their products and services in Canada.

Canadian Professional Sales Association (CPSA)
655 Bay Street, Suite 400
Toronto, ON M5G 2K4

Canada
(888) 267-2772
Web site: http://www.cpsa.com
This association is Canada's leader in developing and serving
sales professionals by providing programs and benefits that
help them sell more and sell smarter.

Manufacturers' Agents National Association (MANA)
16-A Journey, Suite 200
Aliso Viejo, CA 92656
(877) 626-2776
Web site: http://www.manaonline.org
This association of interdependent manufacturers and representatives is dedicated to protecting and promoting sales of
wholesale goods through the manufacturer-sales rep channel.

National Association of Professional Insurance Agents (PIA)
400 North Washington Street
Alexandria, VA 22314
(703) 836-9340
Web site: http://www.pianet.org
The PIA educates agency owners and staff about insurance
concepts, keeps agents informed about changing company
offerings, and advocates for agents in legislative matters.

National Association of Realtors
430 North Michigan Avenue
Chicago, IL 60611-4087
(800) 874-6500
Web site: http://www.realtor.org
The National Association of Realtors represents more than
one million members involved in residential and commercial real estate. It works to preserve the free enterprise
system and the right to own, use, and transfer property.

National Automobile Dealers Association (NADA)
8400 Westpark Drive
McLean, VA 22102
(703) 821-7000 or (800) 252-6232
Web site: http://www.nada.org
The National Automobile Dealers Association provides education, guidance, and training programs to improve
dealership business operations, sales, and service practices.

Radio Advertising Bureau (RAB)
1320 Greenway Drive, Suite #500
Irving, TX 75038
(800) 232-3131
Web site: http://www.rab.com
The Radio Advertising Bureau works to enhance the percep-
tion of radio as a primary medium for advertisers and to
increase radio's advertising and marketing revenue.

WEB SITES

Due to the changing nature of Internet links, Rosen Publishing
has developed an online list of Web sites related to the subject
of this book. This site is updated regularly. Please use this link
to access the list:

http://www.rosenlinks.com/EC/Sales

for further reading

Allan, Jennifer. *If You're Not Having Fun Selling Real Estate, You're Not Doing It Right.* Dothan, AL: Bluegreen Books, 2010.

Allan, Jennifer. *Sell with Soul: Creating an Extraordinary Career in Real Estate Without Losing Your Friends, Your Principles, or Your Self-Respect.* Denver, CO: Bluegreen Books, 2008.

Azar, Brian, and Brad Fenton. *Sales 101: The ReadyAimSell 10-Step System for Successful Selling.* Hollywood, FL: Simon & Brown, 2012.

Carey, Chantal Howell, and Bill Carey. *Make Money as a Buyer's Agent: Double Your Commissions by Working with Real Estate Buyers.* Hoboken, NJ: Wiley, 2007.

Cichelli, David. J. *Compensating the Sales Force: A Practical Guide to Designing Winning Sales Reward Programs.* 2nd ed. New York, NY: McGraw-Hill, 2010.

Hamilton, Dan. *Perfect Phrases for Real Estate Agents and Brokers.* New York, NY: McGraw-Hill, 2009.

Hastings, Jeff. *So You Want to Be an Insurance Agent.* 2nd ed. Scottsdale, AZ: Farmers Career Center, 2009.

Kinder, Jack, Jr., and Garry Kinder. *Secrets of Successful Insurance Sales.* Wise, VA: The Napoleon Hill Foundation, 2012.

Kolah, Ardi. *The Art of Influencing and Selling* (Guru in a Bottle). Philadelphia, PA: Kogan Page Limited, 2013.

Mears, Lee. *How to Become a Travel Agent.* London, England: ExtenzaLife Ltd., 2012.

Mintzer, Rich. *Start Your Own Travel Business and More* (StartUp Series). Irvine, CA: Entrepreneur Press, 2011.

Pierre, Melvin Sr. *Increase Your Insurance Sales, Retention &*
Referrals Now!!! Bloomington, IN: Authorhouse, 2009.

Pink, Daniel H. *To Sell Is Human: The Surprising Truth About*
Moving Others. New York, NY: Penguin Group, 2012.

Porter, Dave, and Linda Galindo. *Where Winners Live: Sell*
More, Earn More, Achieve More Through Personal
Accountability. Hoboken, NJ: Wiley, 2013.

Riley, Daniel. *How to Get A Medical Device Sales Job.* Seattle,
WA: CreateSpace, 2011.

Schiffman, Stephan. *The 25 Sales Habits of Highly Successful*
Salespeople. Avon, MA: Adams Media, 2008.

Theobald, Theo. *On Message: Precision Communication for the*
Digital Age. Philadelphia, PA: Kogan Page Limited, 2013.

bibliography

Allied Real Estate Schools. "Real Estate License Requirements." Retrieved February 2013 (http://www.realestatelicense.com/real-estate-license-requirements.aspx).

Baskin, Jonathan Salem. "Hurricane Sandy Will Be the Biggest Branding Event for Insurance Companies in 2013." Forbes.com, December 4, 2012. Retrieved February 2013 (http://www.forbes.com/sites/jonathansalembaskin/2012/12/04/hurricane-sandy-will-be-the-biggest-branding-event-for-insurance-companies-in-2013).

Bureau of Labor Statistics. "Advertising Sales Agents." *Occupational Outlook Handbook, 2012–13*. Retrieved February 2013 (http://www.bls.gov/ooh/sales/advertising-sales-agents.htm).

Bureau of Labor Statistics. "Insurance Sales Agents." *Occupational Outlook Handbook, 2012–13*. Retrieved February 2013 (http://www.bls.gov/ooh/sales/insurance-sales-agents.htm).

Bureau of Labor Statistics. "Loan Officers." *Occupational Outlook Handbook, 2012–13*. Retrieved February 2013 (http://www.bls.gov/ooh/business-and-financial/loan-officers.htm).

Bureau of Labor Statistics. "Personal Financial Advisors." *Occupational Outlook Handbook, 2012–13*. Retrieved February 2013 (http://www.bls.gov/ooh/business-and-financial/personal-financial-advisors.htm).

Bureau of Labor Statistics. "Real Estate Brokers and Sales Agents." *Occupational Outlook Handbook, 2012–13*. Retrieved February 2013 (http://www.bls.gov/ooh/sales/real-estate-brokers-and-sales-agents.htm).

Bureau of Labor Statistics. "Retail Sales Workers." *Occupational Outlook Handbook, 2012–13.* Retrieved February 2013 (http://www.bls.gov/ooh/sales/retail-sales-workers.htm).

Bureau of Labor Statistics. "Travel Agents." *Occupational Outlook Handbook, 2012–13.* Retrieved February 2013 (http://www.bls.gov/ooh/sales/travel-agents.htm).

Bureau of Labor Statistics. "Wholesale and Manufacturing Sales Representatives." *Occupational Outlook Handbook, 2012–13.* Retrieved February 2013 (http://www.bls.gov/ooh/sales/wholesale-and-manufacturing-sales-representatives.htm).

Cichelli, David J. *Compensating the Sales Force: A Practical Guide to Designing Winning Sales Reward Programs.* New York, NY: McGraw-Hill, 2010.

Edgar, Davey. "New York State Salesperson Exam Practice Quiz." ProProfs Quiz Maker. Retrieved February 2013 (http://www.proprofs.com/quiz-school/quizshow.php?title=new-york-state-real-estate-salesperson-practice-quiz_1&quesnum=7&showNextQ=no).

Guttentag, Jack. *The Mortgage Encyclopedia: The Authoritative Guide to Mortgage Programs, Practices, Prices, and Pitfalls.* 2nd ed. New York, NY: McGraw-Hill, 2010.

MyMajors.com. "Career: Personal Financial Advisor." Retrieved February 2013 (http://www.mymajors.com/careers-and-jobs/Personal-Financial-Advisors).

Plante, Jeff. "Pharmaceutical Sales Job Description—What You Need to Know." EzineArticles.com. Retrieved February 2013 (http://EzineArticles.com/428204).

Pocock, John. "Calm After Calamity: Insurance Protects Farms When Disaster Strikes." FarmIndustryNews.com, February 5, 2013. Retrieved February 2013 (http://farmindustrynews.com/business/calm-after-calamity-insurance-protects-farms-when-disaster-strikes).

Rheault, Scott. *The Sales Interview: Step-by-Step Guide for Sales Candidates: Pharmaceutical-Biotech-Medical-Surgical (Volume 1)*. Seattle, WA: CreateSpace, 2012.

Smith, Jacquelyn. "The 10 Best Companies for Commission-Based Jobs." Forbes.com, May 9, 2011. Retrieved February 2013 (http://www.forbes.com/sites/ jacquelyn-smith/2011/05/09/the-10-best-companies-for-commission-commission-based-jobs).

Tyrell-Smith, Tim. "How to Choose a Career That's Best for You." *U.S. News & World Report*, December 6, 2010. Retrieved February 2013 (http://money.usnews.com /money/ blogs/outside-voices-careers/2010/12/06/how-to-choose-a-career-thats-best-for-you).

Weinberg, Mike. *New Sales. Simplified: The Essential Handbook for Prospecting and New Business Development*. New York, NY: AMACOM, 2013.

index

ABOUT THE AUTHOR

Mindy Mozer is a writer and editor living in Rochester, New York, with her husband and two children. She has also written *Getting a Job in Automotive Care and Service* and *Social Network–Powered Education Opportunities.*

PHOTO CREDITS

Cover (figure) © iStockphoto.com/jsmith; cover (background), p. 1 LuckyPhoto/Shutterstock.com; pp. 4, 14–15 Christian Science Monitor/Getty Images; pp. 8, 27, 36–37, 42–43, 45, 60 © AP Images; pp. 10–11 Jupiterimages/Goodshoot /Thinkstock; p. 16 Boston Globe/Getty Images; pp. 20–21 Ron Chapple Studios/Thinkstock; pp. 22–23 Scott Olson /Getty Images; p. 24 Bloomberg/Getty Images; pp. 30, 49, 57 Joe Raedle/Getty Images; pp. 32–33 Jupiterimages/Brand X Pictures/Getty Images; p. 35 AFP/Getty Images; p. 40 Kansas City Star/McClatchy-Tribune/Getty Images; p. 46 Colorado Springs Gazette/McClatchy-Tribune/Getty Images; p. 50 iStockphoto/Thinkstock; p. 52 © Robin Nelson/ZUMA Press; p. 54 Jupiterimages/Creatas/Thinkstock; p. 63 © The Palm Beach Post/ZUMA Press; p. 66 BananaStock/Thinkstock; back cover (background) © iStockphoto.com/blackred.

Designer: Matt Cauli; Editor: John Kemmerer; Photo Researcher: Amy Feinberg